MOWING
FARGO

Mowing Fargo

Layout and Design ~ Rick Lupert
Front Cover Photo ~ Janeen Kobrinsky
Back Cover Photo ~ Christina Smith
Section Title Page Photos ~ Rick Lupert and Janeen Kobrinsky
Author's Photo ~ Addie Schonbach

Thanks very much to Robert Wynne for his invaluable editorial guidance. (Even though he is a hippy who should cut his hair.) Also thanks to Jamie O'Halloran and Amélie Frank for knowing just what to do with apostrophes and not being afraird to tell about it.

Special thanks to Sacred Beverage Press for publishing the original version of this book in 1998.

(818) 305-4457
or
15522 Stagg Street, Van Nuys, California 91406
or
Rick@PoetrySuperHighway.com
or
http://PoetrySuperHighway.com/

ISBN 978-0-9727555-0-4 $8.00
Third Edition, First Printing ~ August 2016

Contents

Introduction

"Why Fargo" you may ask. And I say, you might as well ask "Why oxygen? Why watermelon? Why cats? Why monkeys? Why Sartre? Why candles? Why french fries? Why the I-Ching?" There are many questions which could be asked. Few, if any, will be answered in this book. But I will say this. Damn straight Fargo. And you may ask "Why 'damn straight Fargo.'" And I say, you may as well ask "Why damn anything that could be damned in a damnable situation; such as fill in the damn blank." And you may ask "Why fill in blank." And I say you might as well not fill in any blank and see where that gets you. Nowhere far I'd bet. Certainly not more than a few blocks away from where you are now. And you know what that means. You know what it's like a few blocks away. You've been there. You like it where you are. I don't have to tell you about the difference between there and where you are now. And that is exactly what I am talking about. The difference. Yes, the difference. Not the sameness. It is not same. It is far from same. It different. (is) And so I went to Fargo on a plane. I could take a bus. It is much less expensive if you buy twenty one days in advance. I could drive. But the ice. And so there was the plane. The Fargo, North Dakota airport is not big. You could find your keys there easily if you lost them. Who wants to lose their keys though? I didn't lose mine. But maybe someday I will. You should have my friends the Kobrinskys over for dinner. They will pay. They're that kind if people. Would that all people could be that kind of people. Norweigan. Canadian. North Dakotan. The way music makes Christina weep. She is a world.

Uff Da.

*To Janeen and Christina;
a couple of women who would make you
want to write a book about Fargo too.*

FARGO, NORTH DAKOTA

More Flags Than Normal

There are Five American Flags
in front of the Fargo, North Dakota Airport.
This is in case
one of them breaks
or you forget
you're not in Canada
anymore.

TeaPeas

I am served Indian Spiced tea
at a party in Fargo
The tea is from Oregon,
the source of all Indian beverages.
I finish the drink and find
two frozen peas
at the bottom of the glass.
I show them to the drink server
and she dances out of the room
chanting giddily
"Fargo, North Dakota . . .
a vegetable in every beverage!"

Urine Overheard

I overhear a Fargo woman
saying soon someone will collect her urine
for twenty four hours.
Whoever she is talking to asks
"how are they gonna get it out"
and she answers
    "I dunno, I suppose they'll slit my neck."
I am tempted to ask
if they have peeing here in Fargo.

A Lot of Salsa

At Juano's mexican food restaurant in Fargo
the waitress brought so many bowls of salsa
we had to finish our lunch in Minnesota.

At the Fargo Cork restaurant

a sign out front proudly boasts
"Beef and Booze."
I don't drink.
I'm a vegetarian.
But Sarah used to work there,
so I thought it was worth mentioning.

Horny's

Hornbacher's is one of the markets in Fargo.
Everyone refers to it as "Horny's."
(for obvious reasons)
Another market is the Sunmart.
But I hear it's no Horny's.

Take My Check, Please

In Fargo
you can write checks at restaurants,
gas stations,
and movie theatres.
They never check your ID.
Unlike in Los Angeles
where they shoot you dead
for even walking out of the house
with your checkbook.

The Great White North

In Fargo, North Dakota,
everyone refers to Canada as
The Motherland.
Even the Norwegians.

The Prairie

Fargo is surrounded by The Prairie
Fields of wheat
Fields of sunflowers
stretching so far
they would make the one at home
on my balcony
weep

Slow Eyed Jeff

Christina and I sit in First Avenue club in Downtown Fargo.
Jeff with the hat and slow eyes sits with us.
She tells him I am from Los Angeles.
After a lengthy silence he says
"It hailed in Los Angeles."
I ask him when, thinking I've missed some
big news back home.
Jeff thinks with his slow eyes and replies
"The late eighties. It must have been the late eighties.
It was probably 1989."
I ask Jeff how he got to Fargo from L.A.
He tells me that he lived on the streets
and then did some time in San Francisco
where he met someone
who gave him a ride
to Oklahoma.

Mowing Fargo

I sit on the John Deere
in the backyard
having a great time
There is nothing to mow
in Los Angeles

The Kobrinskys

Janeen Kobrinsky is Your Mother

Janeen Kobrinsky is my patron
and from what I can tell
the most famous person in Fargo.
She is an artist
and the mother of Sarah.
(who I've already mentioned)
Janeen is also the mother of
many other children,
some of whom she's birthed.
It seems all you have to do is
show up at her house on the Red River
and she'll start to buy shirts and food
for you too.

The Second Floor Kobrinsky Toilet

No one ever flushes
the second floor Kobrinsky toilet.
The floating horrors
one finds become less surprising
as the days progress
and the Kobrinsky boys
mill about in the hallway
bumping into each other muttering
It's not me
It's not me

Janeen Kobrinsky II

My friend Janeen Kobrinsky
runs a small nation.
Everyone knows her by name.

Sarah Kobrinsky

Sarah is a writer from Fargo.
She also dances.
Sarah has worked at every business in the town.
It's part of the town charter.
All new establishments must employ
Sarah Kobrinsky for at least one week.
Sarah is well taken care of here.

The Future of Photography

Sarah needs to go to the ninety-minute photo place
before she leaves for Canada.
Feeling all big city sophisticated,
I share with her the wonders
of sixty-minute photo developing.
Before I can beam too much
she tells me they have a five-minute photo place.

I imagine there must be a place
that has your photos done
before you even shoot them.
A restaurant where you walk in
and they immediately hand you the check and a mint
because your dinner has already been eaten,
and it was good.

Leah Kobrinsky

I

Worships Michael Jackson
Is suspicious of me
Doesn't think I'm a believer

I moonwalk through her living room
Trying to show her
I'm all about Michael

She is still skeptical
I may need a nose job
to gain her confidence

II

Leah organizes a birthday party
for Michael Jackson
He doesn't show
Leaving Leah alone
in a house full of Fargo Birthday Cake
and frosted letters reading
"Happy 40th Michael"

III

You should be a rock star
I say to Leah Kobrinsky.
"I know," says Leah.

Yehudah Kobrinsky

Every morning Hudi Kobrinsky
eats half a bowl of marshmallow Frootloops
collects money from his mother
and leaves the house with nefarious friends
in mysteriously parked cars,
leaving the empty bowl for Janeen to clean up.

I want to write him off for this.
But Janeen tells me how he's sweet
crawling into her bed
with his blanky
every time Nathan is away.

The Widdow Man

The youngest Kobrinsky is Zach.
He is paranoid.
Wasp Invasions.
He lectures us about the differences
between bees, wasps, and hornets,
proudly stating that hornets have two abdomens.

Every few minutes he runs outside
clutching a rolled up newspaper and shouts
     "Are they here yet?!
     Are they here?"

Nathan Kobrinsky

The waitress asks Nathan Kobrinsky
if he would like anything to drink.
"Life Insurance,"
says Nathan Kobrinsky.

CHRISTINA

Prairie Hospitality

You are driving me through the Prairie,
  gravel roads
  fields of harvestables
  and the occasional structure
  made by human beings.
I am miles from anything I know
and even farther from home.

You have worked this land,
know it intimately.
So when you stop the car
(In the middle of somewhere, I'm sure)
and say "I think we should make out now"
I can only assume
it's the right thing to do.

I Am In Fargo for Five Days

After only two,
I am already used to
waking up in your arms.

Treehouse Summit

Christina takes me to her parents farm in Valley City.
We climb into the tree house and encounter
her eight-year-old half brother Jake, and a friend.
They are DRAWING UP PLANS.
They can't talk about it.
"If there's anything I can do," I say, "let me know."
Jake asks if I have a lot of guns.
I tell him "no"
and exit the tree-house
down the slide.

I Am Served Home Cooked Prairie Meal

Food is different on the farm, I think.
As if Christina's mother invented broccoli
just for me.

Sunflowers

Christina takes me
into a field of sunflowers.
Everything I've ever wanted
surrounds me,
holds my hand.

Close Call

You are glad you put your dress back on
before the farmer chased us out of the field.
I am glad for you too.

Driving Fargo

Christina lets me drive her car home one night.
Lesson one:
> Red lights
> mean the same thing
> everywhere.

Learning the Cha-Cha

Driving down University Avenue in Fargo
listening to AM radio
      lounge music
      holding hands
You ask me if I want to learn how to Cha-Cha
Soon the car is stopped
and we are doing the Cha-Cha on the street
in front of Janeen's house
Right, Left
      one two three
Left, Right
      one two three
I would like to learn
all your moves

Fargo North Dakota, California

You are eager
to spend the night with me
in my patrons home.
Makes me want to
install a Fargo, North Dakota
back home
in Los Angeles.

I fell in love in Fargo

It's a hell of a town.

Remembering How To Shower

Thirty years showering by myself
You'd think I'd remember how to do it
But back home
after five days with you
I stare at the soap
wondering how to apply it
without your hands

Two-time Pushcart Prize nominee Rick Lupert has been involved in the Los Angeles poetry community since 1990. He was awarded the Beyond Baroque Distinguished Service Award in 2014 for service to the Los Angeles poetry community. He served for two years as a co-director of the non-profit literary organization Valley Contemporary Poets. His poetry has appeared in numerous magazines and literary journals, including The Los Angeles Times, Rattle, Chiron Review, Red Fez, Zuzu's Petals, Stirring, The Bicycle Review, Caffeine Magazine, Blue Satellite and others. He edited the anthologies Ekphrastia Gone Wild - Poems Inspired by Art, A Poet's Haggadah: Passover through the Eyes of Poets, and The Night Goes on All Night - Noir Inspired Poetry, and is the author of eighteen other books: Romancing the Blarney Stone, Professor Clown on Parade, Making Love to the 50 Ft. Woman, The Gettysburg Undress (Rothco Press), Nothing in New England is New, Death of a Mauve Bat, Sinzibuckwud!, We Put Things In Our Mouths, Paris: It's The Cheese, I Am My Own Orange County, I'm a Jew. Are You?, Feeding Holy Cats, Stolen Mummies, I'd Like to Bake Your Goods, A Man With No Teeth Serves Us Breakfast (Ain't Got No Press), Lizard King of the Laundromat, Brendan Constantine is My Kind of Town (Inevitable Press) and Up Liberty's Skirt (Cassowary Press), and the spoken word album "Rick Lupert Live and Dead" (Ain't Got No Press). He hosted the long running Cobalt Café reading series in Canoga Park for almost twenty-one years and has read his poetry all over the world.

The author on his thirty-fourth birthday with a special hat and a lizard.

Rick created and maintains Poetry Super Highway, an online resource and publication for poets (PoetrySuperHighway.com), Haikuniverse, a daily online small poem publication (Haikuniverse.com), and writes and occasionally draws the daily web comic Cat and Banana with Brendan Constantine. (facebook.com/catandbanana) He also writes the weekly Jewish poetry blog "From the Lupertverse" for JewishJournal.com

Rick works as a music teacher at synagogues in Southern California and as a graphic and web designer for anyone who would like to help pay his mortgage.

Rick's Other Books and Recordings

Romancing The Blarney Stone
Rothco Press ~ August, 2016

Professor Clown on Parade
Rothco Press ~ August, 2016

Rick Lupert Live and Dead (Album)
Ain't Got No Press ~ March, 2016

Making Love to the 50 Ft. Woman
Rothco Press ~ May, 2015

The Gettysburg Undress
Rothco Press ~ May, 2014

Ekphrastia Gone Wild (edited by)
Ain't Got No Press ~ July, 2013

Nothing in New England is New
Ain't Got No Press ~ March, 2013

Death of a Mauve Bat
Ain't Got No Press ~ January, 2012

The Night Goes On All Night
Noir Inspired Poetry (edited by)
Ain't Got No Press ~ November, 2011

Sinzibuckwud!
Ain't Got No Press ~ January, 2011

We Put Things In Our Mouths
Ain't Got No Press ~ January, 2010

A Poet's Haggadah (edited by)
Ain't Got No Press ~ April, 2008

A Man With No Teeth
Serves Us Breakfast
Ain't Got No Press ~ May, 2007

I'd Like to Bake Your Goods
Ain't Got No Press ~ January, 2006

Stolen Mummies
Ain't Got No Press ~ February, 2003

Brendan Constantine is My Kind of Town
Inevitable Press ~ September, 2001

Up Liberty's Skirt
Cassowary Press ~ March, 2001

Feeding Holy Cats
Cassowary Press ~ May, 2000

I'm a Jew, Are You?
Cassowary Press ~ May, 2000

Lizard King of the Laundromat
The Inevitable Press ~ February, 1998

I Am My Own Orange County
Ain't Got No Press ~ May, 1997

Paris: It's The Cheese
Ain't Got No Press ~ May, 1996

For more information:
http://PoetrySuperHighway.com/